Night Animals

Written by Louise Spilsbury

Collins

We go to sleep at night.

2

Some animals feed at night.

A bat flies at night.

It has big ears to hear in the dark.

A bushbaby runs up trees at night.

It has big eyes to see in the dark.

A raccoon looks for food at night.

It has long fingers to feel in the dark.

A coyote hunts at night.

It has a long nose to smell in the dark.

We wake up in the morning.

Some animals go to sleep in the morning!

In the dark

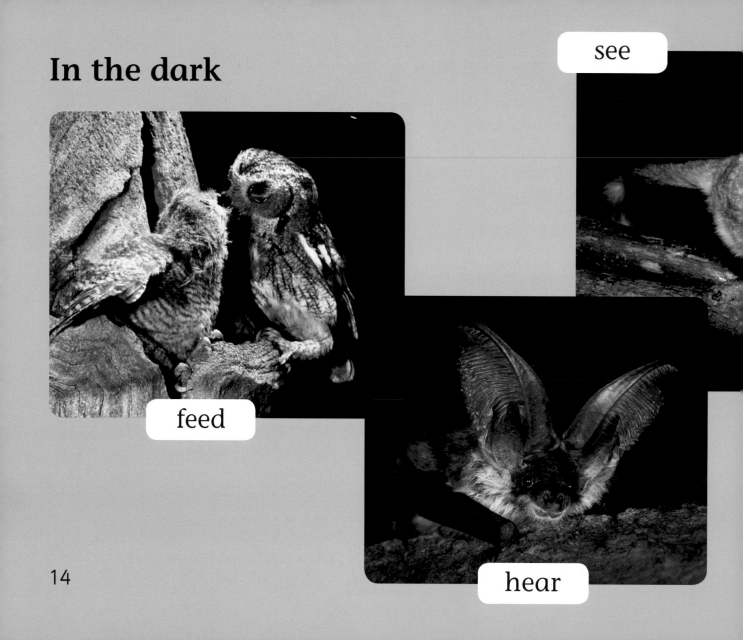

see

feed

hear

smell

feel

Ideas for reading

Written by Clare Dowdall PhD
Lecturer and Primary Literacy Consultant

Learning objectives: read more challenging texts; recognise automatically an increasing number of familiar high frequency words; use syntax and context when reading for meaning; find specific information in simple texts; take turns to speak, listen to others' suggestions and talk about what they are going to do

Curriculum links: Science: Plants and animals in the local environment

High frequency words: when, some, just, out, what, has

Interest words: night, animals, sleep, waking, feed, bat, ears, hear, dark, bushbaby, eyes, see, raccoon, fingers, feel, coyote, nose, smell

Resources: whiteboard, ICT

Word count: 86

Getting started

- Ask children if they know about and have seen any animals that wake up at night time, e.g. bats, hedgehogs, owls.

- Write on the whiteboard the names of animals that the children will be reading about, e.g. bat, bushbaby, raccoon, coyote. Help them to read the names.

- Look at the front cover together. Ask children to try to identify the animal from the list on the whiteboard.

- Read the title and the blurb aloud and discuss why some animals might wake up at night time and what they do when they wake up.

Reading and responding

- Read pp2–3 together. Ask children if this will be a story or an information book and how they can tell.

- Look at the photograph on p3. Ask children to explain what is happening in the picture.